AUSTRALIA

LETTERS FROM AROUND THE WORLD

Margot Richardson

Photographs by Chris Fairclough

CHERRYTREE BOOKS

LETTERS FROM AROUND THE WORLD

Titles in this series

AUSTRALIA · BANGLADESH · BRAZIL · CANADA · CHINA · COSTA RICA · FRANCE · INDIA · INDONESIA · ITALY · JAMAICA · JAPAN · KENYA · MEXICO · PAKISTAN · SPAIN

A Cherrytree Book

Conceived and produced by

Nutshell MEDIA

Intergen House
65–67 Western Road
Hove BN3 2JQ, UK
www.nutshellmedialtd.co.uk

First published in 2004 by
Evans Brothers Ltd
2A Portman Mansions
Chiltern Street
London W1U 6NR

VISIT OUR WEBSITE
www.evansbooks.co.uk
Evans

© Copyright Evans Brothers 2004

Editor: Katie Orchard
Designer: Tim Mayer
Map artwork: Encompass Graphics Ltd
All other artwork: Tim Mayer
Series consultant: Jeff Stanfield, Geography Inspector
  for Ofsted
Literacy consultant: Anne Spiring
All photographs were taken by Chris Fairclough

Acknowledgements
The authors would like to thank the Hulme family, and
the principal, staff and pupils of Stanmore Public School,
Sydney, for all their help with this book.

British Library Cataloguing in Publication Data
  Richardson, Margot
    Australia. – (Letters from around the world)
    1. Australia – Social life and customs – Juvenile
    literature
    2. Australia – Geography – Juvenile literature
    I. Title
    994'.07

ISBN 1 8423 4218 5

Cover: Harriet with her brother, Nicholas, and friends
  Victoria and Max, in front of the Sydney Harbour Bridge.
Title page: Harriet and her friend Olivia belong to a surf
  life-saving club at Bondi beach.
This page: A view over the centre of Sydney.
Contents page: Harriet holds a pumpkin she has grown.
Glossary page: Harriet and her dad meet a koala at the zoo.
Further information page: Harriet's class works on a project
  about Aborigines.
Index: Harriet has a horse-riding lesson.

Printed in China.

Contents

My Country

Saturday, 3 January

33 Boronia Street
Stanmore
Sydney
NSW 2048
Australia

Dear Jo,

G'day! (This is how some Australians say hello. It's short for 'Good day'.)

My name is Harriet Hulme and I'm 9 years old. I live with my family in Sydney, the biggest city in Australia. I have two sisters, Kate, who's 12, and Charlotte, who's 5. I also have a brother, Nicholas, who's 7. I can't wait to help you with your school project on Australia.

Write back soon!

From
Harriet

Here's my family. I'm in front (in the red top) with Nicholas. At the back, from left to right, are Mum, Charlotte, Dad and Kate.

Australia is a huge island, called a continent. Most Australians live on the strip of coast that starts at Melbourne and runs up past Sydney to Brisbane.

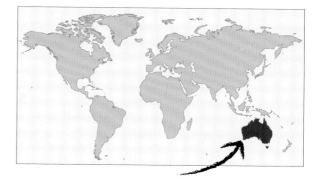

Australia's place in the world.

0   200   400   600   800 kilometres

0   200   400 miles

Timor Sea

Darwin

Torres Strait

N

Coral Sea

INDIAN OCEAN

NORTHERN TERRITORY

GREAT BARRIER REEF

GREAT DIVIDING RANGE

GREAT SANDY DESERT

QUEENSLAND

PACIFIC OCEAN

Uluru
△(Ayers Rock)

SIMPSON DESERT

WESTERN AUSTRALIA

GREAT VICTORIA DESERT

Lake Eyre

SOUTH AUSTRALIA

Brisbane

GREAT DIVIDING RANGE

Perth

Darling

NEW SOUTH WALES

Adelaide

Leeton

Murray

Sydney

CANBERRA

△Mount Kosciuszko
2,229m

VICTORIA

Melbourne

AUSTRALIAN ALPS

Tasman Sea

TASMANIA

Australia is the sixth-largest country in the world.

5

The centre of Sydney was built around a large, natural harbour. The first people to live there were the Aborigines, Australia's indigenous people.

In 1788, people from Britain arrived in ships and started to build a small town. Over the next 200 years, Sydney grew into a busy, modern city. Now, more than 4 million people live there.

Sydney's famous landmark is the Opera House. Its roof looks like the sails of a ship.

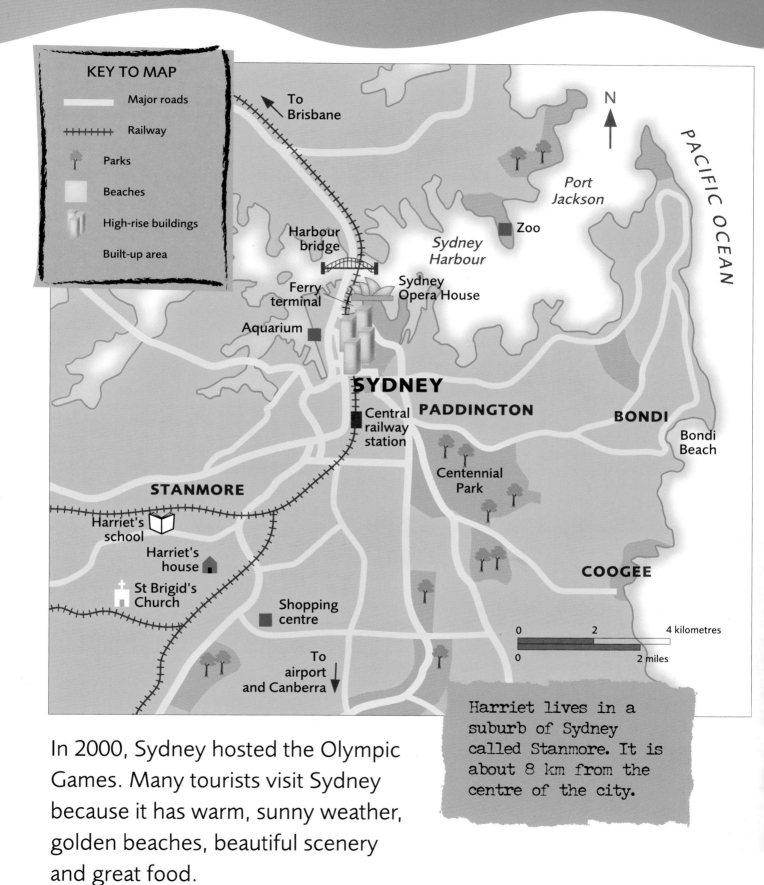

KEY TO MAP

⎯⎯⎯	Major roads
++++++	Railway
🌲	Parks
▪	Beaches
🏢	High-rise buildings
	Built-up area

To Brisbane

Harbour bridge

Ferry terminal

Aquarium

Zoo

Port Jackson

Sydney Harbour

Sydney Opera House

SYDNEY

Central railway station

PADDINGTON

BONDI

Bondi Beach

Centennial Park

STANMORE

Harriet's school

Harriet's house

St Brigid's Church

Shopping centre

COOGEE

To airport and Canberra

PACIFIC OCEAN

N

0	2	4 kilometres
0		2 miles

In 2000, Sydney hosted the Olympic Games. Many tourists visit Sydney because it has warm, sunny weather, golden beaches, beautiful scenery and great food.

Harriet lives in a suburb of Sydney called Stanmore. It is about 8 km from the centre of the city.

Landscape and Weather

The east coast of Australia is warm and wet. The centre of the country is desert, and it is mostly hot and dry. The north is very hot and humid, and has fierce storms called cyclones. In the south there are mountains called the Australian Alps, where it snows in winter.

Harriet and her friend, Olivia, belong to a surf life-saving club. They wear special caps so they can be seen easily in the sea.

In Sydney the hottest months are December, January and February, and the coolest are July and August.

Most Australians live by the coast. Bondi Beach, in Sydney, is the perfect place for relaxing and surfing in the waves.

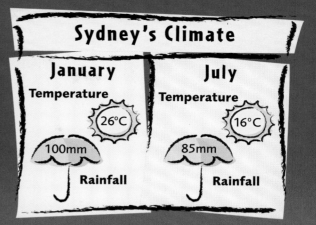

Sydney's Climate

January	July
Temperature 26°C	**Temperature** 16°C
100mm **Rainfall**	85mm **Rainfall**

At Home

Like most people in Sydney, Harriet's family lives in a house with a garden. Stanmore is one of the older parts of Sydney. Many of the houses here were built more than 100 years ago, which is quite old for Australia.

Harriet's house has a veranda, which gives shade in hot weather.

Harriet's house has four bedrooms, two bathrooms, a living room, a dining room, a kitchen, and a study, which Harriet's dad uses for work.

Harriet sometimes reads to Charlotte before they go to bed.

Harriet shares a bedroom with her sister, Charlotte. Kate and Nicholas each have a room of their own.

Harriet's family plays a board game in the living room.

11

The back garden is just big enough to fit in a trampoline.

Harriet's house is near the centre of the city, so the garden is not very big. A lot of the houses further away from the city centre have large gardens. Many houses even have space for a swimming pool.

Harriet feeds her pet cat, Tigger, in the garden.

Friday, 16 April

33 Boronia Street
Stanmore
Sydney
NSW 2048
Australia

Dear Jo,

I enjoyed reading about your house. We have a vegetable patch in our garden. We grow tomatoes, carrots, spinach, broccoli, beetroot, corn, pumpkins and some herbs. In summer, when it's really hot, we have to water them every day.

I like the pumpkins best. They have a hard skin and are orange and sweet inside. We eat pumpkin with a roast dinner, mashed like potato, or made into soup. It's yummy!

From
Harriet

Pumpkins grow on a vine.
This one is big and heavy,
but it's not ripe yet.

Food and Mealtimes

For breakfast Harriet usually has cereal with milk, toast with a yeast spread called Vegemite, and some fruit juice.

Harriet takes a packed lunch to school. She has a honey or Vegemite sandwich, some fruit, a drink and a home-made biscuit or cake.

On warm mornings, Harriet's family eats breakfast outside in the garden.

Australian people used to eat mainly plain meat with vegetables. Now foods from all around the world are popular.

In the evenings, Harriet's family may have pasta, a stir-fry with chicken, roast lamb or fish and chips.

Harriet's mum buys most of the family's food at the supermarket.

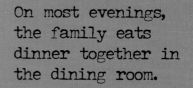

On most evenings, the family eats dinner together in the dining room.

15

Harriet's family has
a Chinese meal in
Sydney's Chinatown.

On special days, such as
birthdays, Harriet's family
eats out in a restaurant.
There is a huge choice
of restaurants: Thai,
Vietnamese, Chinese,
Greek, Italian, African
and Indian.

In the summer, the
family sometimes has a
barbecue in the garden.

Sunday, 13 June

33 Boronia Street
Stanmore
Sydney
NSW 2048
Australia

Dear Jo,

You asked for a typical Australian recipe. Here's how to make Anzac biscuits. We often make them.

You will need: 100g rolled oats, 150g plain flour, 120g sugar, 60g desiccated coconut, 1 tablespoon golden syrup, 100g butter, 1/2 teaspoon bicarbonate of soda, 1 tablespoon very hot water.

1. Mix the oats, flour, sugar and coconut in a large bowl.
2. Ask an adult to help melt the syrup and butter together in a pan.
3. Mix together the soda and hot water. Add the butter and syrup.
4. Add this to the dry mixture in the bowl, and mix well.
5. Place tablespoonfuls of the mixture on the greased baking tray.
6. Bake in the oven at 150°C (Gas Mark 2) for 20 minutes.

I hope you like them!

From

Harriet

Here I am putting balls of the biscuit mixture on to a baking tray.

School Day

Harriet goes to a school near her home. It takes about 5 minutes to get there by car. There are 420 boys and girls at Harriet's school, from 5 to 12 years old.

At Harriet's school, everyone wears school uniform, including a special hat to protect them from the sun.

There are 30 children in Harriet's class. They are having a reading lesson.

In Harriet's art class, the children learn about Aboriginal paintings, and try the style for themselves.

School starts with assembly at 9 a.m. and finishes at 3 p.m. Harriet studies English, maths, science and technology, drama, history, geography, scripture, music, art and sport. Harriet's favourite subject is drama.

There are ten computers in Harriet's classroom and a computer centre in the school library.

19

Some of these children are playing cricket in the school playground.

Harriet's school has three playgrounds and a grassy playing field. The children play softball (which is a bit like baseball), cricket, netball and soccer.

On warm afternoons after school, Harriet does her homework outside.

Some children have after-school classes. They sing in the choir, or play in the school band. Others learn ballet or tennis.

Monday, 14 September

33 Boronia Street
Stanmore
Sydney
NSW 2048
Australia

Dear Jo,

Ni Hao! (You say 'nee how'. It means 'hello' in Mandarin.)

There are many people from other countries living in Australia. The three main groups living in our area speak Greek, Mandarin, or Portuguese. Each week, everyone at our school has a lesson to study the different countries and their languages. Sometimes, we cook some of their foods or learn traditional dances.

Are you learning any other languages?

From

Harriet

This is my Mandarin class. Mandarin is one of the languages spoken in China.

Off to Work

Harriet's mum is a deputy principal (deputy headteacher) at a high school. She works all day, from 8.30 a.m. to 5.30 p.m.

Harriet's dad is a vet. He has a shorter working day so that he can pick up the children from school and be with them at home in the afternoons.

Harriet's dad works with animals to keep them healthy.

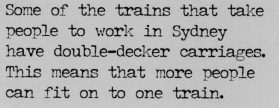

In Sydney, many people work in offices, shops and restaurants. They travel to work by car, or on trains that take people in and out of the centre of the city.

Some of the trains that take people to work in Sydney have double-decker carriages. This means that more people can fit on to one train.

These Italian women run a pizza restaurant near Harriet's home.

Free Time

When all Harriet's schoolwork is done, she likes reading, playing with her friends and watching television. She also goes swimming, plays netball and rides her bike.

Koalas are native Australian animals. It is hard to find them in the wild, so most people see them in zoos.

Harriet has lessons to improve her riding. She always wears a helmet to protect her head if she falls.

Harriet's grandparents live on a farm about 7 hours' drive from Sydney. In the school holidays, the whole family goes to stay there. When Harriet is visiting her grandparents, she enjoys horse-riding.

Australians love sport. Cricket, surfing and football are all popular.

These people are playing a game of touch rugby on the beach while others swim and surf in the sea behind.

Religion and Festivals

Most Australians are Christian, but many of them do not often go to church. Harriet's family is Catholic. On Sunday mornings Harriet and her mum go to their local church, called St Brigid's.

A Sunday morning service at St Brigid's Church, where Harriet goes with her mother.

Greek and Chinese Christians have their own churches. There are also many Buddhist centres and temples in Sydney.

At Easter, Greek Christians have a parade, to mark the day that Jesus rose from the dead.

Wednesday, 29 December

33 Boronia Street
Stanmore
Sydney
NSW 2048
Australia

Dear Jo,

Thanks for my Christmas card! In Australia, Christmas comes during our long summer holiday. Even though it's hot outside, we still put up Christmas trees and have decorations with pretend snow!

This year we spent Christmas Day at home and had a traditional roast turkey dinner with plum pudding for desert. Last year, we were at my grandparents' farm, where we celebrated with my dad's huge family – there were 43 of us! It was 40°C outside, so we had an Australian lunch of prawns, cold meats and salads.

From

Harriet

This is me finding my presents under the tree on Christmas morning. I was given a portable CD player, a board game, and a new boogie board and flippers.

Fact File

Capital city: Canberra is a modern city that was specially built for Australia's national parliament.

Other major cities: Sydney, Melbourne, Brisbane and Perth.

Size: 7,686,850km^2

Population: 19,600,000

Indigenous population: The first Australians, the Aborigines and Torres Strait Islanders, have lived in Australia for about 50,000 years. They make up 2 per cent of Australia's population. (The first European people settled in Australia just over 200 years ago.)

Flag: Australia's flag includes the Union flag, to show that Australia is part of the British Commonwealth. It also has five white stars to show the Southern Cross, a pattern of stars that can be seen in the Australian sky. The large, seven-pointed star represents the states and territories of Australia.

Currency: The Australian dollar, made up of 100 cents.

Main religions: Christianity. Other religions include Islam, Buddhism, Judaism and Hinduism.

Stamps: Australian stamps often show native animals, plants and flowers, like the ones below. Others have photos of landscapes, sports, festivals and famous Australians.

Languages: English is the main language. However, 24 per cent of people living in Australia were born in other countries, or have parents from other countries. The other languages spoken most are Italian, Greek, Cantonese, Arabic and Vietnamese.

Main industries: Manufacturing (food and machinery) are big industries, and so are business and finance. Agriculture and coal mining are also important.

Longest river: Murray River (2,589km)

Highest mountain: Mount Kosciuszko (2,229m). It is found in the Australian Alps, in southern New South Wales.

Australian wildlife: Most of Australia's native animals are not found in any other countries. These include animals that raise their young in pouches on their bodies, such as the koala, kangaroo (shown below) and possum. Others are the only mammals that lay eggs, the platypus and the echidna.

Glossary

Anzac Anzac stands for Australia and New Zealand Army Corps, which was the force that fought in the First World War. Anzac biscuits were named after these soldiers because Australians were very proud of them.

Aborigines The first people who lived in Australia. They were the only people living there until people from Britain settled in 1788.

Christian Someone who follows the teachings of Jesus Christ.

continent A big, continuous expanse of land. Europe, Africa, Asia, North America, South America, Australasia and Antarctica are continents.

cyclone A fierce storm with very strong winds.

desert Dry land with very little water.

harbour A place on a coast where ships can shelter.

humid Damp or moist.

indigenous Coming from a particular place. This is the word that Australian Aborigines use to describe themselves.

native A plant or animal that was born in, or belongs to, a particular place.

scripture The Australian name for learning about religion, mainly Christianity.

stir fry A way of cooking where meat and vegetables are cut into small pieces and fried quickly. Chinese and Thai foods are often cooked in this way.

suburbs The areas on the edges of a city, where most people live.

surf Waves breaking on a beach.

Vegemite A type of dark, salty spread made from concentrated yeast extract. It is very popular in Australia.

veranda A roofed area on the outside of a house, usually on the ground floor.

Further Information

Information books:

Continents: Australia and Oceania by Mary Fox (Heinemann Library, 2003)

Next Stop Australia by Fred Martin (Heinemann Library, 1998)

Living in Australia by Ruth Thomson (Franklin Watts, 2002)

Picture a Country: Australia by H. Pluckrose (Franklin Watts, 2001)

Websites:

Australia
www.australia.com
Information for tourists.

Visit NSW
www.visitnsw.com.au
Tourist information on New South Wales.

Zootopia
www.zo.nsw.gov.au
A zoo website with information about native animals.

Aboriginal Art Online
www.aboriginalartonline.com/
Pictures of traditional and modern art by Aboriginal people.

Stanmore Public School
www.stanmore-p.schools.nsw.edu.au/
The website of Harriet's school, including details of festivals celebrated and a kids' forum.

Index